One Day in Paradise

retold and illustrated by Helme Heine

A Margaret K. McElderry Book
ATHENEUM   1986   NEW YORK

Published originally under the title: *Samtag in Paradies* by Gertraud Middelhauve Verlag, Köln   Copyright © 1985 by Gertraud Middelhauve Verlag, Köln   Translation copyright © 1986 by Atheneum Publishers, Inc.   All rights reserved   Composition by Boro Typographers, New York, New York   Printed in Germany   Bound by Bookbinders, Inc., Jersey City, New Jersey   Library of Congress catalog card number: 85-72492   ISBN 0-689-50394-6   First American Edition

In five days, God created
the heavens and the earth.
The first day, He kindled
the light and separated it
from the darkness.

The second day, He built
the heavens.

The third day, He formed
the earth and the sea,

and He designed all the plants
and laid out a garden.

The fourth day, He hung up in the sky the sun,
the moon and the stars.

And on the fifth day, He began to model the animals.

One Day in Paradise

retold and illustrated by Helme Heine

Early in the morning of the sixth day, He finished making the living creatures.

For five long days He had been sawing, hammering and painting, making plans and changing them again. He had calculated, written and drawn, measured and weighed.

Now His house was empty. It had grown quiet, and God decided to have a little rest.

Only human beings were still to be created,
and this great task He had left to do last. He
intended to create a being that looked like
Him, as a child looks like its father.

God went to fetch the clay from the field,
added water and kneaded it until it was soft.
His work could now begin.

First He modeled the feet, for God wanted His human being to stand firm and steady. The legs came next so the being could walk through life upright. The body, which held everything together, followed; then two arms and two hands for working, and, finally, a head for thinking.

The human being grew more and more like
God. He gave it two eyes to see the beauty of
Paradise and a nose to smell the fragrant air of

Paradise and two ears to hear God and a mouth
to tell about the wonders of the world and a
heart, a big heart, to love His creation.

When He saw that His work was good, He
formed a second human being.

To both of them He granted an immortal soul, breathed life into them and called them Adam and Eve.

He gave them Paradise as a gift.

At night God watched over their sleep. Content
with what He had made, He looked forward to
the seventh day, the day of rest.

A Margaret K. McElderry Book
ATHENEUM PUBLISHERS

D